As I See It

The dyslexic's view of the world, in writing and pictures

Dyslexia Institute

WALKER BOOKS
LONDON

What Is Dyslexia?

Dyslexia affects about one in every twenty-five people – that's one child in every classroom.

In order to be able to read, write, spell and do number work effectively a child has to combine all the individual skills of learning into the one complex skill of being able to read and write accurately. A dyslexic child has specific learning difficulties which obstruct the organization of the individual skills.

To illustrate what this means, imagine a filing cabinet containing hundreds of papers, filed in individual slots but without labels. So when specific information is sought, it is impossible to find that information because it is not organized properly.

Being dyslexic is rather like this: in the same way that a filing cabinet needs to be organized and labelled by the person who is to use it, so too does the learning system for a dyslexic.

This is why it is essential that dyslexics should be recognized and helped when they are young enough – before they start to fail and lose confidence in themselves. If they are not given that appropriate help they will almost certainly under-achieve in school and probably in later life.

Dyslexics have difficulties, but they also have abilities. Many of them have creative talents and are potential actors, architects, artists, computer and electronic experts, designers, engineers, entrepreneurs. They have a different kind of learning ability. If they can't learn the way they are being taught, then they must be taught the way they can learn.

What is the Dyslexia Institute?

The Dyslexia Institute was established in 1972 to ensure the identification and teaching of dyslexics and the training of their teachers, and to offer advice and further people's knowledge about dyslexia. It is the only national network in the world offering this range of help.

Since the Dyslexia Institute first began teaching, it has developed learning programmes to build the organization of skills into a learning process for each student. Firstly individual weaknesses and abilities are assessed, then a structured teaching programme is designed which involves memory training, exercises to correct specific weaknesses in auditory and visual perception and in hand skills. By building a cumulative structure of learning geared to the individual student's needs, their confidence will improve and they will cope with learning in school.

Dyslexia affects people irrespective of background or intelligence, and provision is costly. The Dyslexia Foundation Bursary Fund was established in 1981 to ensure that those needing help should not be denied it.

The royalties from this book will go to the Dyslexia Foundation Bursary Fund.

A Letter from Susan Hampshire

I think the most important step for youngsters with specific learning difficulties today is to be properly assessed as soon as possible and then have expert specialist teaching. That is why the Bursary Fund is so vital. Many parents who are not able to pay for these lessons can call on the Bursary Fund which supports 150 students (more if their coffers are full) to subsidize their child's lessons and thus prepare them to face the future with hope.

Over the years I have travelled up and down the country to the various Dyslexia Institutes and met many children, some when they have only just been assessed. At this stage the children have been withdrawn, lacking in confidence and too shy to talk to me. When visiting that same centre six months later the same children come bouncing up with smiling faces, full of confidence, to tell me of their progress. The change is so overwhelming that I know the special teaching offered by the Dyslexia Institute is the key to dyslexic children having a happy, fulfilled life.

Sadly there are still many children needing help at the Dyslexia Institute's 20 centres and 49 outposts or in 41 school centres, and regrettably there is not enough money to subsidize them. The need is so enormous; money runs out more quickly than it comes in. It is heartbreaking to think of the children who would be helped if only the resources were available. Lack of money is coming between them and the future they deserve.

Susan Hampshire
Patron of the Dyslexia Institute Bursary Fund

The "As I See It" Competition

Every year the Dyslexia Institute holds a competition for dyslexic children and adults, on the theme of "As I See It".

In 1989, entrants were invited to explore a choice of six topics:

1) Through the eyes of a dyslexic
2) Disaster!
3) Beneath the surface
4) "I was only trying to help..."
5) A visit to the zoo, fair or theme park
6) As I see it ... a personal view

These could be interpreted in four separate categories:

a) writing
b) poetry
c) art
d) photography

Anyone who had been identified as dyslexic was eligible to enter, without penalty for standards of writing or spelling.

There were three categories:

10 years and under
11 - 15 years
16 years and over (including adults)

The judges were:

Raymond Briggs
Roy Castle
Patrick Lichfield
Chris Mallet
Bill Oddie
Helen Rollason
George Spanswick

This book presents a selection of the best entrants in the four categories, and together they provide a unique insight into the dyslexic's view of the world and his or her difficulties within it.

Winners

POETRY

16 years and over

1st	Hannah Batten	Age 17	Haywards Heath College
2nd	Miss H. Atkins	Age 24	Bury St Edmunds D.I.
3rd	Simon Cundy	Age 16	Shapwick Senior School

11-15 years

1st	Jean-Paul Garcia	Age 12	Ellesmere College
2nd	Matthew Hopkinson	Age 14	Coventry D.I.
3rd	Kathryn Janes	Age 13	Derby D.I. (Fairfield School)

10 years and under

1st	Johnathen McKay	Age 9	Derby D.I. (Foremarke Hall)
2nd	Graham Stewart	Age 10	Glasgow D.I.
3rd	Michael Davison	Age 10	Lincoln D.I.

ESSAYS

16 years and over

1st	Roy Wilcox	Age 65	Potishead
2nd	Christine Zair		Bedford
3rd	J.E.Ringer	Age 19	Bloxham School

11-15 years

1st	John Doughty	Age 11	Stone D.I.
2nd	Amy Hope	Age 11	Wessex Dyslexia Tutors Group
3rd	Michael Crouch	Age 12	Berkshire Dyslexia Assn.

10 years and under

1st	Elizabeth Revell	Age 10	Hawkhurst Court Dyslexia Centre
Joint 2nd			
	Gemma Ellis	Age 9	Helen Arkell Centre (Frensham)
	Gareth Richey	Age 10	Winchester D.I.

PHOTOGRAPHY

16 years and over

1st	Maria Parnell	Age 16	Rugby & District D.A.
2nd	Philip Bedford	Adult	Barts Dyslexia Unit
3rd	Lynda Middlemast	Adult	Southampton

11-15 years

1st	Tim McAlpine	Age 12	Stone D.I.
2nd	Desmond McShane	Age 15	Ipswich D.I.
3rd	Emma Greaves	Age 13	Sheffield D.I.

10 years and under

1st	Christopher Graham	Age 9	Bracknell D.I.
2nd	Stuart Castle	Age 10	Portishead D.I.
3rd	Benjamin Graves	Age 10	Fairley House School

ART

16 years and over

1st	Quinton Brooks	Age 16	Sidcot School
2nd	Paul Southerland	Adult	Medway Dyslexia Centre
3rd	Charlotte Parkes	Age 16	Sheffield D.I.

11-15 years

1st	Stuart Tweddle	Age 11	Darlington D.I.
Joint 2nd			
	James Waite	Age 12	West Wickam D.I.
	Carolynne Ireland	Age 11	Sutton Coldfield D.I.

10 years and under

1st	Michael O'Sullivan	Age 10	Eversley D.I.
Joint 2nd			
	Leanne Brush	Age 10	Northern Ireland D.A.
	Tom Sturges	Age 10	Bath D.I.

The judging panel for the written entries, seated: Raymond Briggs, Susan Rollason, Roy Castle, with the editor from Walker Books behind. Regrettably it was not possible to include in this book all the winning entries, especially the photographs and pictorial winners, because of problems in reproduction.

CONTENTS

As I See It

My Problem

When they said that I was dyslexic it came as a bit of a shock. Because the other girls and boys were different and not like me. I knew that I was clever but somehow it wouldn't come out, my pencil and paper were strangers don't you see.

James Lee Daniels (9)

Letters

Adam Brown (9)

Beneath the Surface

(original spelling)

I have blond her, Blue eys and an infeckshos smill. Pealple tell mum haw gorgus I am and is ent she looky to have me. But under the surface I live in a tumoyl. Words look like swigles and riting storys is a disaster area because of spellings. There were no ply times at my old school untill work was fineshed wich ment no plytims at all. Thechers sead I was clevor but just didn't try. Shouting was the only way the techors comuniccatid with me. Uther boys made fun of me and so I beckame lonly and mishroboll. it was like being jon a decert island lost and alone. Life was life and sckooll was sckool. Tings cangd when I moved to my new sckooll. I am the same inside new as I am out side. I can not reed and spell, well all most. I have frens and the teckhors all most never shout. They treet me as an intellejent person and not a zomby. I wish I new my fythor. I wonder wot will hapon to me when I have to leve. Will my in side sty the same as my out side. Wat will be Beneath my Surface. I wish I new.

Alexander Parsonage (9)

As I See It

Avoiding School

Tim McAlpine (12)

Through the Eyes of a Dyslexic

When I was younger, about four, I was in my first class and the teacher kept on telling me off for doing things wrong that the other children didn't get wrong. One day the teacher told us to do a collage and to cut out a mouse but I cut out the mouse from the paper for the back of the collage. I got a very big shaking and a big smack. I was so frightened I wet my knickers.

When I was a bit older in a higher class the Headmaster just said that I daydreamed. I didn't understand the work anyway. I thought that my reading was as far as I should have got. I used to get my b and d the wrong way round. Whenever I went up to the teacher to ask a question she always said "Go and sit down, I have no time for you."

I never had any friends because I could not read and write. I had sort of given up all hope in being able to read and write and get any friends. When I went to another school, a dancing school, absolutely everyone hated me there.

After every weekend, on the Monday back to school I used to cry because I had lost a book or something like that, because I was afraid of the teachers telling me off.

Then I came to the school I am at now and all the teachers understand about our Learning Difficulties and all the girls in the school do like me, that is about 7 girls.

There is one very horrible thing I hate, the most is not to be able to sit down and read a good book.

As I See It

I wish I could read books which tell me how to make things.

Elizabeth Revell (10)

Not Another Debit for My Homework!

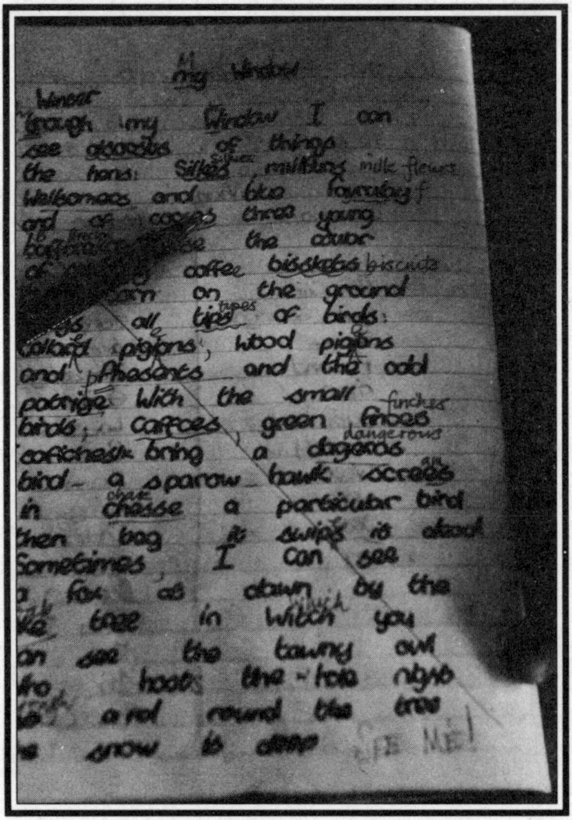
My Window
See Me!

Jonathan Bennett (11)

Through the Eyes of a Dyslexic

"So, I've got a disease, ha?"

"No," said my mum, "You haven't got a disease."

We were walking across the market square. I had just spent three hours in a hot stuffy old building doing a bunch of tests to figure out why I had trouble with things like reading and spelling. It was extremely boring and I thought stupid, but I kept myself from breaking because I found the coolest escape route. It was a series of drainpipes and landings outside the window that I almost put to the test.

"So what does it mean, am I really thick or something?"

"No, just the opposite, the tests say you're really smart."

By this time I was ready to scream.

"So why can't I do maths and things as fast as the other kids?"

"Because you're a dyslexic."

"Isn't there a medicine to make it better?"

"No, we can't just make it go away, but we're going to send you to some classes which will teach you some tricks to overcome dyslexia."

"I don't want to go to any dumb classes! And I don't want to be dyslexic!"

Well, I did go to those classes. I think the first term was a disaster. I went to an old dusty building that made me step back in time with a terrible echo. It was like a nightmare, and I still didn't want to know about being dyslexic.

As I See It

In fact I didn't want anyone to know I was dyslexic, especially my friends. Some of them were really nice about it, but some laughed at me. It really made me want to punch them in the face, but I didn't. I cried myself to sleep a lot. My mum and dad helped with things like homework and stuff, but I hate those little blue cards.

In September I changed classes and met Mrs Bently, but I could never remember her name, so she wrote it on my hand. I thought it was pretty cool, because I am not allowed to write on my hands! I don't know when it happened, but things must have just clicked. By March I was up to my own level in writing and reading. In fact my school teacher said that I was doing so well he was surprised that I was still going to the classes.

My mum said I should keep going because my brain's capable of doing even more than my age says I am. I know that some really smart people are dyslexic, and I don't think that I'm any Einstein or anything and some days I get really fed up because things don't make sense. But as I see it, being dyslexic isn't going to stop me doing anything or being anyone I want to be when I grow up.

Justin Hydes (10)

Trapped

O
A
R
b
???
L
T
U
U
C

Richard Marsh (10)

As I See It

Cars

Fiat, Ferrari, Ford Fiestas
   Renaults and Rovers rolling by
Minis motoring down the street
   Pink ones, yellow ones, red ones too.
I've got a white one, how about you?

Lotus, Lancias, Ladas too
   Some have four doors,
Some have two.
   We've got six doors, how about you?

Dave's got a Carlton, a Mini too,
   Pat's got a Renault
which is blue.
   I've got a Rover, how about you?

Cars of the future,
   Cars of today,
I've got a new one,
   So they say.

Michael Davison (10)

The Planets

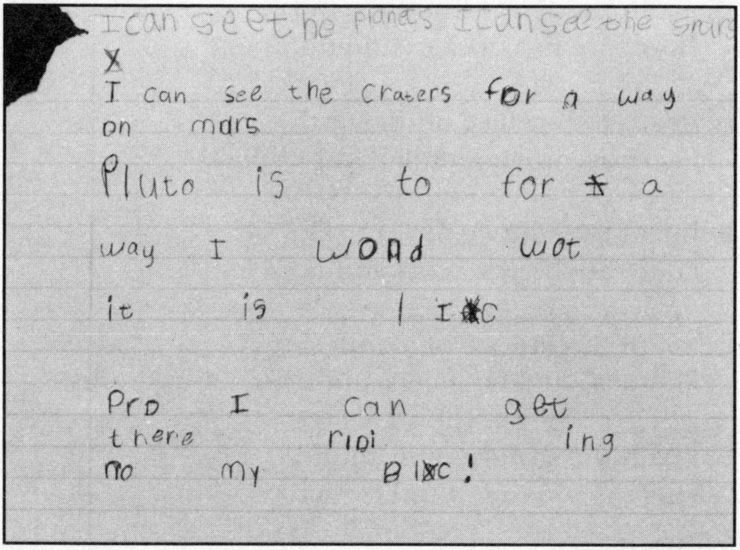
Icanseethe planets Icansee the stars
X
I can see the craters for a way
on mars
Pluto is to for a
way I wond wot
it is lIc
Pro I can get
there ridi ing
no my Blc !

I can see the planets, I can see the stars,
I can see the craters far away on Mars.
Pluto is too far away, I wonder what it's like.
Perhaps I can get there riding on my bike.

Edward Johnson (7)

Beneath the Surface

Beneath the surface of the water
There are fish, whales and dolphins.

Beneath the surface of the earth
There are worms, moles and rabbits.

Beneath the surface of your skin
There are bones, veins and muscles.

Beneath the surface of a quilt
There is a teddy, sheets and a hot water bottle.

Beneath the surface of my mind
There is winning, thinking and working.

Johnathen McKay (9)

Beneath the Surface (a stone)

I was picked up, and thrown into the pond. There were so many ripples and bubbles, as I floated to the bottom. As I went, I saw fish and tadpoles glare at me. I landed with a bump, I'm afraid, on a very fat and angry stone. He rolled over, and I landed on the other side. I looked up and the ripples had gone, but there were lots of drops of something. I think that it might be rain but I wasn't sure. Whatever it was, it made a nice sound.

I really wish that I hadn't been thrown into the pond, because it's so grimy in the water, but the tadpoles like it anyway.

There were lots of tiny little insects swimming around. I wish some of them swam down to me, because it's so misty, and I want them out of the way, and also I'm very hungry.

This great big hand came into the pond, and lifted me out, and I was put back in my place. The girl that threw me in got a telling off from her dad, because I was a very important part of the garden.

Jane Colborne (13)

As I See It

Crocodile

The cool cruel crocodile
was cruising down a creek,
He met a magical mandarin
and ate him head to feet.

The cool cruel crocodile
was running out of time,
He ate a clock to speed him up
and now he's feeling fine.

Mary Turner (10)

As I See It

W. A. Middleton (adult)

My Sister Is Handicapped

My sister is handicapped and I knew this when she was born, and I was scared. Everybody looked at her in hospital when they came to visit someone else, just because she had a big head. That was because of the fluid in her head. When we took her home from the hospital she never stopped crying for about six months. She didn't stop crying day and night. When my dad knew she was handicapped, he said "this is your fault" to my mum and left. That upset me. We asked the hospital people if she would ever be mobile and they said, "She will never sit up, she will never feed herself and she will never walk." When she was four years old she got whooping cough and she was rushed to hospital. There were healthy children in hospital dying of whooping cough and I was scared that my sister might die, but my sister did not stop fighting and she did not die. When we go shopping people stare at my sister just because she's handicapped. A grown-up man fell over my sister because he kept staring at her. I think this happens because people don't understand. Me and my mum love my sister very much and we treat her just like us. My sister beats me up but that's just her way of loving me. She can now sit up, feed herself, and she can nearly walk and talk, and that wouldn't be possible except by me, my mum, my nan and my grandad, and we love Jodie very much. So if you see a handicapped person don't stare, give them help, like help carry the wheel chair up the stairs. Even if it is only hello, that could make their day. If people were more caring, handicapped people would feel safer.

John Doughty (11)

As I See It

I Was Only Trying to Help

It hasn't been a good day,
   in fact one of the worst.
Mummy said I've been a pest.
   Daddy's only cursed.
I didn't think the dog was too pleased either
   and sister only cried.
It wasn't my fault really.
   I was only trying to help.

I brought the dog in from his walk,
   and sat him in the hall.
I washed him down with the hose.
   It wasn't my fault really
that he jumped up on the chair.
   I was only trying to help.

I wanted to help Dad in the garden.
   So I thought I would fetch the wheel-barrow.
It's really his fault he parked so close.
   It was only a tap, a little scratch,
right across the door.
   It wasn't my fault, really,
I was only trying to help.

I came in from the garden,
   I thought I'd need a wash.
It's not my fault my memory's bad and I
   forgot the tap.
I thought I heard a little drip,
   upon the kitchen floor.

It wasn't my fault really,
  I was only trying to help.

The kitchen needs re-decorating.
  I think it did before.
I was feeling rather hungry,
  so I cooked chips for us all.
The frying pan caught fire,
  the smoke just filled the room.
It wasn't my fault really,
  I was only trying to help.

James Salverson (10)

Disaster

Happy Birthday to you Happy Birthday to you. Happy Birthday Dear Mum & Happy Birth-day to You.
Mum!

James Waite (12)

Disaster

I lay in bed, hands behind my head, staring moodily at the ceiling. Rain pattered against my windows and the noise of traffic filtered through from outside. But my mind was concentrated on something else – my stomach. It was empty and rumbling like a volcano, and it was my brother's fault. I wondered if Oliver could feel the waves of hatred aimed directly at him, or Mum and Dad too for that matter. After all, it was my brother's glass of ribena that did the damage.

It all started when the little tyke kicked me under the table on my shins. Naturally I kicked him back. My jerking knee lifted the corner of the table and sent his ribena flying. Smack, it hit the newly decorated kitchen wall, and left a stain that reminded me of one of those modern art paintings. Unfortunately, Mum is not a lover of modern art. My brother and I sat in tense silence, waiting for the storm to break, and sure enough it did like a ton of bricks.

"Whose ribena was that?" yelled Mum. "His" we both said automatically. "Then you can BOTH go to bed," said Mum, clearly very angry. We departed to our bedrooms in silence, stomping as loudly as we dared up the stairs.

This had been an hour ago, and now I was absolutely starving. Oliver had deprived me of my supper. Then I remembered the chocolate chip cookies in the larder downstairs. I decided to take a chance. I crept out onto the landing and stopped to listen for sounds of activity from below. I heard the sound of the television droning in the background and now and then an outburst of laughter from one of my parents. It sounded like a fun programme. With any luck it would hold their attention.

I took a deep breath and began to descend the stairs, remembering to miss out the creaky one, third from the bottom. I sneaked past the open living room door and into the kitchen. The tiled floor felt cold on my bare feet. The fridge gave out one of those eerie shudders, making me jump. I could feel my heart racing as I reached for the biscuit tin. Grabbing a handful I stuffed some in my pockets for later, the remaining two I popped into my mouth. I was about to make my get-away when I heard my mum's voice.

"Oh no, not Derek Jameson. I'll go and make a cup of coffee." My heart froze. I thought frantically for a hiding place. Click, the kitchen light snapped on.

"What are you doing here?" Mum said. "Sleep walking," I said hopefully, spitting biscuit crumbs across the room. "That does it, no pocket money this week." "But Mum," I wailed dismally. I stomped back up the stairs, and lay down in bed still hungry. I thought back on the evening's events. What a disaster!

Michael Crouch (12)

Disaster

Disaster!

Nicholas Russell (9)

All Led to Its Death

It was running fast as shot,
Made sprays of dust beneath it,
The panting of its breath,
Its trail of blood,
All led to its death.
The killers were behind it now,
Shot made sprays of dust behind it,
The panting of its breath,
Its trail of blood,
All led to its death.
Brambles are cutting it,
Shot made sprays of dust behind it,
The panting of its breath,
Its trail of blood,
All led to its death.
The hunter pulls his trigger,
It's dead.

Benedict Mason (11)

Beneath the Surface

W. A. Middleton (adult)

As I See It

Karnt Spel

Yu may nott no,
    Yu may nott sea,
Thut speling wurds
    Is nott foor me.

I carnt spel "katt"
    And "dogg" and "whool"
And az foor "booc",
    Imm-pos-e-bull!

And ther are wurds
    Thut are kwite ard,
Lik "ellefunt"
    and "kredit kard".

All mi boocs hav
    Lotz off misstacs,
Thisz givs the staf
    Sum bigg hedakes.

But thers a wurd,
    Yu'll sea itt kleer,
Thiz is the won,
    "DYS-LEX-I-A!"

Kathryn Janes (13)

Jumbled Jungle of Reading

WORK WORK
A E I O U
READ READ READ
Sprite
Colonel
ERASER
pen•men•hen
bell sell
THGiR ↔ LEFT

Stuart Tweddle (11)

As I See It

The Mind behind the Mask

A man who has a mask to hide his unhappiness,
his fear of the world.
Nowhere to go. No destination to reach,
No friends to comfort him.
He has a mask to divide him from the rest
of mankind.
He tries to communicate,
but no words can escape from his mouth,
as if he was chained in the top of a remote tower.
The fires of his mind keep whirling around
in agony.
No thoughts of life or death.
Can he escape? No, because his brain is locked in
an iron cell, with no key to unlock his worries.

Roger Davis (12)

Beneath the Surface

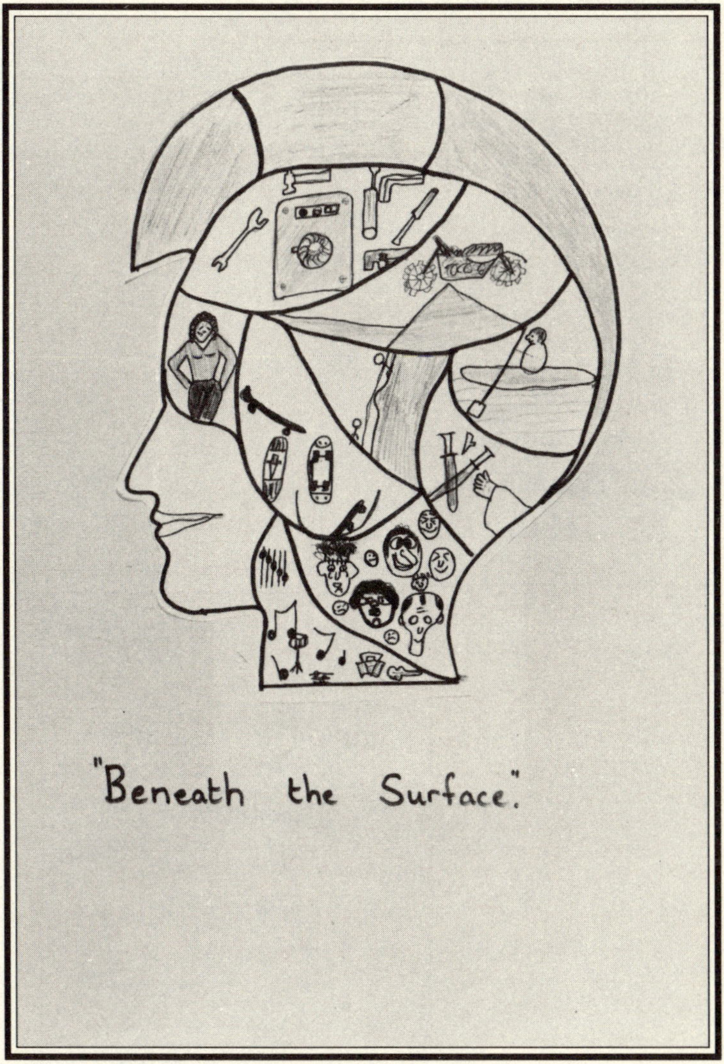
"Beneath the Surface"

Richard Braithwaite (15)

As I See It

As I See It... A Personal View

(the original)

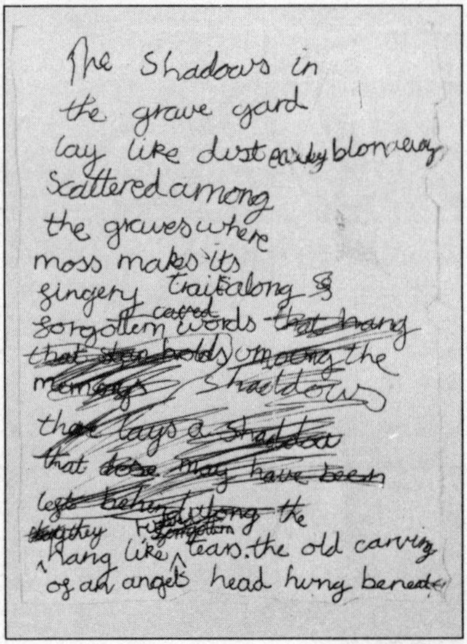
The shadows in
the grave yard
lay like dust easily blown away
scattered among
the graves where
moss makes its
fingery trail along
forgotten carved words ~~that hang~~
~~that stay holds~~ among the
~~memory~~ shaddows
~~that lays a shaddow~~
~~that may have been~~
~~left behind~~ belong the
they hang like forgotten tears. the old carving
of an angel's head hung beneath

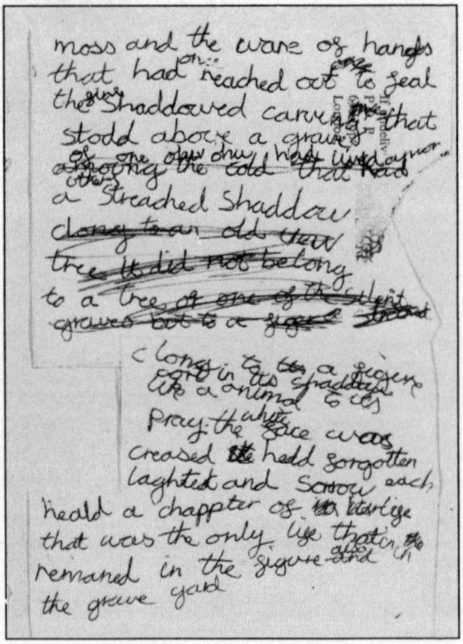
moss and the ware of hands
that had reached out to feel
the shaddowed carving that
stodd above a grave
~~among the cold that had~~
a streached shaddow
~~along to an old~~
~~tree it did not belong~~
to a tree ~~of one of the silent~~
~~graves but to a figure~~
clong to a figure
like a animal to its
pray. the white face was
creased the held forgotten
laghter and sorrow each
heald a chappter of a lifetime
that was the only life that in
remaned in the figure in
the grave yard

The shadows in the graveyard lay like dust,
Easily blown away, scattered among the graves
Where moss makes its fingery trails
Along forgotten words which hang like tears.
The old carving of an angel's head,
Hung beneath moss and the wear of hands
That once reached out to feel the fine
shadowed carving,
Stood above a grave of one who had lived
among others.
A stretched shadow clung to a figure caught
In her shadow like an animal to its prey.
The white face was creased.
It held forgotten laughter and sorrow,
Each held a chapter of her life
That was the only life
That remained in the figure
Also in the graveyard.

Caroline Beck (13)

Me

It was me
In the mirror,
Yes, me.
The eyes
In shadow
The mind
At ease.
Looking deeper,
Deeper,
Now not me
In the mirror,
Not me.
A childish girl
Stared sweetly
A wandering mind
This girl I see.
But as I look
She changes
Quick,
A shy face
Stared slowly
In my eyes
Yes, me in the mirror,
Me.

Lisa Addis (12)

Portrait

Jayne Gardner (14)

As I See It

Sea World

The great shining body left the water like a missile.
Its dazzling black coat shone like polished marble
As it arked through the air in slow motion.
Smack!
The great killer whale thomped the surface,
Sending up a wall of spray like a reverse waterfall
As it entered its modern habitat.

A shrieking cry came from the jolly dolphins,
Showing off their skills,
The athletes of the sea.
The friendly faces charmed the crowd
As they wait for their applause.

The sneaky shark sinuously swam
At a speedy pace,
Its streamline body
Like a giant newt
Its dreadful fin
Like a vicious razor blade.

Silently
The smooth grey sting ray
Calmly glides,
Like a bird of the sea,
An eagle soaring high up
On the coral mountains,
Its shadow on the sand below
A triangular kite,
Trailing its long sharp tail.

In the artificial rock pool
The imaginative forest came to life,
Seahorses galloped
In the bright coral wood.
Timid shrimps darted away to hide
Among the anemone trees.
Sea urchins and starfish
Created a magical fairground
For the creatures of
The Undersea World.

Jean-Paul Garcia (12)

As I See It

Latchmoor

"Latchmoor" – As I see it.
David Edge

David Edge (11)

How I Feel

Pain and confusion, sorrow and sadness,
How do I feel? I don't know.
But the hurt in my head, the Pain in my core,
Is getting unbearably hot.

But worse than all this is the hurt in my heart,
The sadness and shame that I feel.
For those who could help me,
  they're far in the distance,
And can't understand what I cry!

The string in my head is unravelling fast,
And the arrows of Pain hit their mark.
I'm lost in a maze, there's no-one to turn to,
The corners are shut up and dark.

I'm lost in time, the way out is not signed,
And I've forgotten the way I came in.
I've been here before, I must look for the door,
But each step of the way is no use.

How long have I been here, when will it end
I don't know whether it will at all.
I'm stuck in a brew that someone is mixing.
Which witch will give me the cure?

I've been put out to dry, and some bits are missing,
And time will not heal the wounds.
I'll grasp life's line, and follow it through,
To look for the door that is mine.

Hannah Batten (17)

As I See It

The Last Vegetarian Voodoo in Scunthorpe

Quinton Brooks (16)

Under the Surface of the Party Popper

(original spelling)

Meney people beleve that the party poper was first developed in Japan, to add a bit of exitment to a dull partey or selibration, but this in actule fact is falce.

It was first developed by a team of sintists from the british Institute, heded by Dr Melbry, in 1939, as an of shout of the H bom progect; but it was only finaly completed in 1946. To late to be used in the war. Because of the amount of money and efort put into the party poper progect, and the hudge tecnilogicl advances in particl-volocity-potenchl phisics, it was decided an alternative use should be found for this extrodeneryly powfel otomic propelent.

The first move in this progect code, named "pop party", was the development of the PP 1 (Party Poper One). The Party Poper 1 is what we recogoise in the 20th century as the Party Popper. Origenely it was designd on a comershl bases to be sold to rais funds for the further investigations into the pop party progect.

The Institut found after a wile the PP 1 did not rais enough funds for ther progect, and desighed the PP 2. This was revoloshonery for its time and incorperated a kind of duble barled party poper. They also built the PP 3. This, even dy todays standards is the most powful party poper of its kind known to mankind. Unfortynatly the PP 3 never found its way from the test sight, which still egsists though now unused, on the moors at dartmoor becous the force egserted when the three barles wher actovated simultaniosly could have easaly back fired and blown the hed of the firer. The sales of PP 1 and PP 2 proved to bring in ample funds for Dr Melbry. One of Dr Meldrys asistons Mr R.G. Tomas BSc. hit upon the idear in the early 1950 of using the PPP (party poper powder) as part of a dilivery system for the planed cheicl wepon defence system war heds.

This was looked into and was developed. It was code named the Chmical Party Poper. The Chemicl Party Poper Incorperated the highest micro gidence and siloon giro optical procesers systems. In 1955 a new module alinment tecneek was introduced to the Party Poper Powder Paking sequence Known as the PPPP This was caled the Party Poper Powder Phase Packing it was known as the PPPPP. The PPPPP incorperated the principl of phisics in the principl known as the Party Poper Powder Phase Packing Principl, PPPPPP for short.

The Party Poper Power Phase Paking Principl aded an extra 52% to the epishency of the Chemicl Party Poper. After this terific advancm the Chemicl party poper had truly proved it's self as the gratest propolshen agent known in the entire univers and the idear it was a advanced wast of money or an explosif wher over run by the amazing potenchal of its use for the improvment of the quality of life.

In 1953 Dr Melbory was awarded an MBE and the pop party progect was awarded a Queens Award To Industry. Sir Melbory and Richard Gorden Tomas dothe got a nobel prise to since, and three weeks later the progect made an afishel secret.

As the party poper powder in tis nature is very advanced it folows when firing your party poper, ther are some very percific gide lines to folow to acheve the most spectacular reults.

1/To fire for an acurat range imdatween 2 and 12ft one should gust point the firing end of the party poper at the target and fire. If the target is less than 2ft point the party poper at an angle of elivation of 88 60' and in the direction of the target. this give the bonce efect ie. shoutig it up and leting it fall down. If the target is moor than 12ft away one should folow the formular below.

R= maqimum range wished to be acheve
r= minomom range wished to be acheved
W= wind risitens
V= vilocity
A= angle of elivation

$$\frac{W\ (R-r)=A}{V}$$

$$\frac{W\ (R-r)=A}{62.37}$$

2/If it is your wish to obtain geo stationaty orbit from the equatern just fire your party poper at 89 and towards the east.

If you are eney wher els you must folow the above equation.

If you are attempting an extra-atmospheric

launch, that is sending your party popper out of the atmosphere, the most potentially globally catastrophic emergency is a failure to obtain sufficient orbital height, as the party popper, when re-entering the atmosphere, would not burn up and a high nutron proten particle acceleration will result in very high radio-activity. In this case you should follow the below instructions.

1. Inform no one.
2. Lock your front door, draw all curtains.
3. Buy ticket to Australia (because when the world finds out what a complete moron you are and how much pollution, death and destruction you have caused they will probably kill you)

OR IF YOU ARE A SAINT

1. Inform every one
2. Go immediately to the crash sight and cover it in 24,000 tons of sand.
3. Encase the sand in a 25ft thick graphite shield.
4. Encase it in 1,200,000 tons of concrete.
5. Leave it for 10,000,000 years
6. Get 12,000 miles away and stay there fo 10,000,000 years

So remember next time you fire a party popper, you are unleashing the world's greatest power force.

James McEwan (15)

The Sands of Time

I kneel down
    on the beach of time
To steal some sand
    and thus be born.

The mini Sahara,
    imprisoned in fingers.
The small grains cry,
    wanting to escape.

Between tight bars,
    they fall screaming,
Crashing downwards,
    broken arms and legs.

I laugh at their fate,
    powerless to catch them.
They laugh at my fate,
    happy to fall.

I tighten their cage,
    begging them to stop.
Their laughter scares me,
    their waterfall runs away.

I can count the grains,
    I can see their spines,
As disaster strikes;
    I wave goodbye.

William Browne (17)

As I See It

Philip Bedford (26)

Why Kill a Rhino?

Why kill a rhinoceros, just for his horn? The horn is only of compressed hair. An elephant lies dead by a waterhole, his face cut half away just to get at the tusks, which are made of ivory. Tigers are shot just for their coats and many other big cats are shot too, so that vain women and men can wear their skins. Young seal pups are killed in front of their mothers, because man said that they eat all of the fish. Whales have harpoons shot into them; they are killed in their thousands.

Man puts his rubbish into the sea and he is killing fish and plant life. Doesn't he know that if the sea dies, we can die too? The forests around the world are being cleared for building and farmland. The soil from these areas will be washed away within three years, leaving everything barren and dead. The trees are cut down for furniture or they are burnt. The smoke blocks out the sun for days and kills other plants, never to be seen again.

In Germany, Italy, France and North Africa men stand and wait for the migration birds to fly over. They are shot for sport. These men have stone walls that they hide behind to shoot down blackbirds, songthrush, finches and any other birds that are on their migration route.

"10-9-8-7-6-5-4-3-2-1 We have lift off!" Another rocket going up into the outer space. Isn't man brainy that he can get through gravity, yet more than half the world is starving. Man is so involved in war and fighting between different religions that he is not looking at the poor human who is in the middle of it all.

As I see it, man is making a right mess of this planet, what with his unwanted items just thrown in a ditch with no thought to the pollution he is causing. The unnecessary killing of whales, seal pups, rhinoceros, elephants and birds.

I have one acre of land. At one end of this land is a woody part, where we have put five bird boxes up in the trees. All boxes were used this year by blue tits and coal tits. We found in the garage a robin's nest. She had built it in the rolled-up hose from the vacuum cleaner. The robins brought up two families, three in the first, four in the second.

In the hawthorn hedge a blackbird brought up her family of three. In the laden tree a thrush had her nest of youngsters. The sycamore tree had woodpigeons in and the poplars had three families of magpies. The hawthorn hedge between the poplars had more variety of birds in it, as under the hedge at least twelve rabbits live.

Now just look at how many birds and animals live on this one acre of land. So why can't man look after the planet?

He can put a rocket on the moon, but he cannot feed his people.

Sandra Attwood (adult)

Through the Eyes of a Dyslexic

WAY OUT
OV3R BRIOGE
LAOIES

Paul Southerland (adult)

As I See It

As I See It... A Personal View

What is Dyslexia? What is it like not to be able to spell? I do not know as I cannot spell, it all looks the same to me.

I am dyslexic, I always have been, I always will be, but I have never been able to spell so how can I tell you what it is like? I must admit to being at a slight advantage to most dyslexics since I can read. I do not know how I learned, I certainly did not get any help, I just picked it up somewhere along the line. When you have lived with something for the whole of your life you do not possess a before and after experience, you cannot give a rational description. All you can do is relate your experiences.

My first experience of being different was when I was 6. I can remember being at school and starting my first reading book, *Janet and John* Book 1. I can remember all the rest of my classmates moving onto *Janet and John* Book 2,3,4,5, etc but I never moved from Book 1. What did the school say? "Do not worry, he is just a slow learner." SLOW! By the time I was in Class 7, the year before secondary school, I was still trying to read *Janet and John* Book 1. My parents just accepted the problem, or when they tried to help would just get frustrated.

I am luckier than most. My English teacher at secondary school believed that I was not "stupid", and that there was some reason why I was unable to grasp English. She fought an epic battle with the Local Education Authority and finally went directly to the Scottish Education Authority and persuaded them to allow me to dictate my English exam (I became the first person in Scotland to do this; I told you I was lucky) and not to be marked down on other exams. This resulted in a grade move in my O'Levels from D and E to four As, three Bs and one C. I can tell you there were a lot of surprised teachers at my school when they saw these results. Unfortunately I received the same outward disbelief that I had a problem when I went to college. After four years of struggling to compete on an equal par with other students, and spending inordinate amounts of time trying to get my spelling right (the days before word processing), I eventually got my degree, and the highest award the college presented for personal endeavour and achievement. I did not bother to pick it up: what I had needed was their support over the previous four years.

Dyslexia is like most diseases. It is worse in a social group when you have to read out loud or comment on a document that we have all just read. Unfortunately I am still on the first page when the rest have finished, or when you have to write a short note to a colleague and you cannot spell the key word to the sentence, what do you do? Leave the mistake, or try to rearrange the sentence so missing out the word you do not know?

I work as a computer consultant, so the "word" is my tool of trade. The worst problem for me is when working on a large report. My secretary will interpret what I have written and type what she thinks I mean. The problem however is that in the middle of a document you will get a word which is totally out of context and unfortunately I will not be able to notice the mistake. So later on when you are having the report read out, someone will start to laugh because of the word out of context, pointing out the mistake to me. However, I will not notice the error, so miss out in the joke. However a joke is not a joke when there might be 10 mistakes on a page. I am luckier than most, as I have both a supportive wife and colleagues who will proof-read important work for me.

I can read magazines like *Private Eye* but cannot understand the satirical style. However, after many years I have come to terms with my disability. One of the hardest things for me, is watching my son grow up. He is 4 right now, and is learning the alphabet and how to write. I hope he will not inherit my disability, as I would not wish that on anyone else. However, every night I read him a story. But as he is getting older he asks for more elaborate stories, which I cannot read out loud well. The other night he said, "Daddy, will you get Mummy to read to me, she reads a better story." Children can be so cruel.

I am now proud of what I have achieved. If it were not for my disability I might have achieved more. Alas life is not fair. I will tell anyone who will listen that I am dyslexic. I do not feel it is something to be embarrassed about. It is almost something to be proud of.

Scott Matheson (30)

A Tale Told by an Idiot

Can you imagine a hundred or so kids chanting the prayers of "Old father witchart who had a tart in heaven".

Every morning for nine years or so my school days started like this.

Suffer little children; God, it would seem, and the Bristol Education Committee made certain of that, as hour after hour of what seemed to me completely meaningless phrases all the kids at Baptist Senior Mixed sang out in flat unison:

Two twos are four
Four fours are sixteen
Two pecks are one bushel
A pint of water is a pound and a quarter
I before E except after C.

Only a hero or complete idiot would have dared ask what it all meant. The school motto if it had one was scripture and the lash.

Early morning prayers were spent kneeling on the floor of the assembly hall. "Don't fidget, that boy." Wallop! Splinters from the tatty floor made my knees fester, which meant the birds in our garden never got stale bread. Mum used ours to make bread poultice. "Look at you, there's a state to get in," and then my dad would always put in his pennyworth, "little bleeders going rotten." I would explain, "every morning we kneels on the floor and prays for salvation." "I'd rather have a pint and a good cooked dinner, that's my salvation," said Dad. Mum would tut at some of his remarks. Though neither of my parents were what you would call religious, I think they'd both been disillusioned years before.

Mum often said she'd never seen a smile on the face of a corpse even though heaven was just around the corner. Mum was a sort of expert when it came to death, for as well as taking in washing, she'd get in an envelope a tear-stained thank you note and a half a crown for "laying out" which, as my dad put it, was tidying up the poor sod before he or she got planted.

I was still at school when my poor dad got planted himself. I shall always remember being taken to his bedroom, the room was full of steam, and thinking that perhaps our family business was expanding and Dad was taking in washing too. But the steam I found out later was coming from a flat spouted kettle and was to help him breathe. I remember also the awful stench of carbolic which came from a pot under the bed, and a tin bowl by his bedside in which he spat up bits of his lungs.

It was the last time I was to see him and what I saw haunted my dreams for years. My dad's eyes were wild and frightened, as though through the swirling steam he had seen where he was going and didn't like the look of it.

I can see him now lifting himself up and looking around the room as if looking for a way of escape, and in a last choking scream of defiance shouted, "They always tell lies to the poor."

These words have stood me in good stead against the simpering lies of politicians and experts of all kinds!

There aren't any two-headed sheep in Wales and those creepies in the drinking water are completely harmless.

In my war I had the great fortune to be told I was joining a luckly ship, so I immediately put on my lifebelt and waited. It wasn't long before COMRAD VITE looked through his monacle and shouted "Achtung" and my luckly ship blew up and sank like a stone, and I found myself floating in a particularly nasty bone-cracking cold bit of ocean.

You can tell by this where my first and formative years were spent, at the pictures, for I knew all U Boat Captains looked like Comrad Vite, I knew Ronald Colman had discovered India, Paul Mewnie discovered radium, ploughed all good earth and mowed down the hoods on St Valentine's Day.

The cinema also taught us languages: "Viva Matchoes", "Achtung", "Vosist loos" and "Touche" from the greatest swordsman in all France. History, Geography, Morality. The bad guys always wore black hats, the heroes white and the villains always got their come-uppance, no complications, everything was black and white.

Our heroes were 20ft tall, born in lightning and spoke with voices of thunder, and God rode a pinto pony and kids packed like sardines sucked rainbows in the dark.

Besides the cinema our other great treat was a Saturday night trip to Paradise, and the only way to get there was on the top deck of a tram where the tip-up seats snapped at our bottoms like crocodiles as the tram lurched and rattled through the gas-lit streets, sparks from the overhead wires cascaded down over our heads and flashed in the eyeless windows of the houses. A screaching lurching chariot of fire, it flew banners, proclaiming England's Glory, Typhoo Tips, and iron geloids. How we envied the driver dressed in his huge tent-like overcoat with his gauntlet hands gripping the shiny brass handles.

"Castle Street, Castle Street," shouted the conductor, and a hoard of screaching kids poured down the steps from the top deck each one trying to land on the driver's warning bell and at the same time dodging the wild swings of the conductor. "You little bleeders" and a row of little bleeders stuck out their tongues hoping they didn't get the same conductor on the way back.

Clutching our pocket money we joined the crowds in Castle Street, which on a Saturday might turn into wonderland. Both sides of the street were lined with hawkers' barrows loaded with mountains of coloured sweets, pontefract cakes, sherbert sparklers and my favourite huge shiny striped gobstoppers. There were carts of Canary Island bananas, vegetables of all kinds, and pyramids of spit-polished red apples, great bunches of flowers a fanfare of colour for taking to Gran on Sunday.

The pubs were packed to overflowing, the kids on the pavement supping pop and the whole colourful wonderful scene lit by hundreds of carbide-hissing lamps. Who would have thought that this scene was to be no more. In a few short hours in 1942 houses, shops, streets were to disappear in a firestorm.

All this was a long time ago, but my memories come flooding back as though it was only yesterday, but without structure or logic which is like life I suppose.

At the age of 55 I had the good fortune to go to College and it was in this enlightened place that I found out I had dyslexia, so after my first days of schooling having been told I was without hope and an idiot from birth it was a great boost to my ego.

If one suffers from dyslexia one's work must always be filtered through someone else who working with me will straighten out the almost indecipherable gobbledy-gook so that the reader, instead of tut-tutting at the structure of my work, will consider the worthiness of my thought.

Roy Wilcox (adult)

First published 1990
by Walker Books Ltd
87 Vauxhall Walk, London SE11 5HJ

Reprinted 1990

Printed in Great Britain by Richard Clay Ltd,
Bungay, Suffolk

British Library Cataloguing in Publication Data
As I see It.
1. Man. Dyslexia
I. Dyslexia Institute
616.85'53

ISBN 0-7445-1601-3